Creative Patterns 2

Coloring Books For Adults Vol.2

Karim Benyagoub

ISBN-10: 1508450218

ISBN-13: 978-1508450214

www.ingramcontent.com/pod-product-compliance
Lightning Source LLC
Chambersburg PA
CBHW080339290526
45790CB00010B/3762